40 & Fabulous

Pearls of Wisdom

Aishwarya Arun

Dedication

This book is dedicated to all the people who have had an impact on what I am today, and to the Almighty for watching over me.

~ An '84 soul, turning 40

Introduction

Welcome to "40 & Fabulous: Pearls of Wisdom," a collection of insights and lessons gathered over four decades of life.

As a proud member of the 80s generation, born in 1984, I belong to the unique cohort of millennials who have witnessed an extraordinary transformation in technology, culture, and society. From the era of cassette tapes to the age of streaming services, from black and white television sets to high-definition color screens, and from landline telephones to smartphones that connect us instantaneously across the globe, we have experienced a whirlwind of change, unlike any other generation before us.

Turning forty is a milestone that prompts reflection and introspection. It is a time to look back on the journey we have traveled, the challenges we have overcome, and the lessons we have learned along the way. Each experience, whether personal or observed, has contributed to the wealth of wisdom encapsulated in this book. In "40 & Fabulous: Pearls of Wisdom," I aim to share these insights in simple, relatable language, drawing from my own life experiences and the stories of those around me.

This book is not a guide to success or a roadmap to happiness, but rather a collection of reflections and observations that I hope will resonate with readers on their journey through life.

Life is a journey of continuous learning, and the lessons we gather along the way are like precious pearls, each one unique and valuable in its own right. As we navigate the complexities of modern existence, these pearls of wisdom serve as guiding lights, illuminating our path and helping us make sense of the world around us.

Whether you are embarking on your journey into the realm of adulthood, navigating the challenges of midlife, or simply seeking a moment of reflection and inspiration, I invite you to join me on this voyage of discovery. Together, let us explore the timeless truths and enduring wisdom that have shaped our lives and continue to enrich our souls.

So, here's to forty years of laughter, tears, triumphs, and tribulations. May the pearls of wisdom contained within these pages serve as beacons of light, guiding you through the ebbs and flows of life's ever-changing tide.
Welcome to "40 & Fabulous: Pearls of Wisdom."

Let the journey begin.

TABLE OF CONTENT

Embracing Self: A Journey of Self-Acceptance

Self-acceptance is a journey many of us embark on, filled with twists, turns, and unexpected challenges. It's about embracing every facet of ourselves, even the parts we may have once wished to hide. My journey towards self-acceptance began with a childhood marked by a thyroid condition that led to weight gain, teasing, and a constant struggle to fit in.

My Story

As a child, I bore the weight of not just my body but also the burden of others' judgments. "Moti", (which means fat in Hindi), they would call me, their words like stones hurled at my fragile sense of self. Despite the love and support of my family, I couldn't shake off the sting of those taunts. I felt like an outsider, always trying to shrink myself to fit into a world that seemed too small to contain someone like me.

But amidst the darkness, there were rays of hope. My parents became my pillars of strength, reminding me that my worth transcended the limitations others placed upon me. Their unwavering belief in my abilities fueled my determination to excel academically. Despite the hurdles, I soared in my studies, finding solace in the refuge of books and the embrace of melodies.

College ushered in a new chapter, one filled with opportunities for growth and self-discovery. Surrounded by supportive peers and mentors, I began to shed the weight of self-doubt and embrace the beauty of my uniqueness. Music became my sanctuary, a place where I could express myself freely without fear of judgment.

With each passing day, I learned to love myself not in spite of my imperfections but because of them. My journey towards self-acceptance wasn't easy, but it was worth every struggle, and every tear shed along the way. Today, I stand tall, a testament to the power of resilience and the beauty of self-love.

Conclusion
To anyone struggling to find acceptance in a world that often feels unkind, I offer these words of encouragement: You are worthy, just as you are. Your worth is not defined by the number on a scale or the opinions of others.

Embrace your uniqueness, celebrate your journey, and remember that self-acceptance is not a destination but a lifelong process. In the end, it's not about conforming to society's standards but about embracing the beautiful mosaic that is you.

Prioritizing Health: The Cost of Neglect

In a world where priorities often clash, the pursuit of success can sometimes come at the expense of one's well-being. This was a lesson I learned the hard way, as I found myself entangled in the relentless cycle of work, neglecting the very foundation of my existence – my health.

As an ambitious professional, climbing the corporate ladder was my singular focus. Long hours at the office, countless deadlines, and the constant pressure to excel became the norm. In the pursuit of career advancement, I overlooked the subtle warnings my body tried to convey, dismissing fatigue as a by-product of hard work and stress as a necessary evil. Little did I know, this neglect would soon lead me down a path I never imagined.

My Experience
It was a seemingly ordinary day at the office when a sudden wave of dizziness engulfed me, sending shockwaves of panic through my body. Ignoring the discomfort, I pushed through, attributing it to lack of sleep and excessive workload.

But my body had reached its breaking point. What began as a minor inconvenience soon escalated into a medical emergency, landing me in the hospital with a diagnosis that shook me to the core – severe exhaustion coupled with underlying health issues exacerbated by neglect.

As I lay confined to a hospital bed, surrounded by the sterile scent of antiseptic and the incessant beeping of medical equipment, reality dawned upon me with unforgiving clarity. The very pursuit of success I so ardently chased had become the catalyst for my downfall. Each beep of the monitor served as a stark reminder of the heavy toll neglecting my health had exacted upon me.

Conclusion
Emerging from the ordeal, I vowed to redefine my priorities, recognizing that true success encompasses not only professional achievements but also physical and mental well-being. The exorbitant bills that accompanied my hospitalization served as a sobering reminder of the cost of neglect – a price far too steep to pay.

Armed with newfound wisdom, I embarked on a journey of self-care, striking a delicate balance between ambition and health. No longer would I allow the pursuit of success to overshadow the importance of nurturing my body and soul. In the end, it is not the accolades or achievements that define us, but rather our resilience in prioritizing what truly matters – our health.

Embracing Depth: Quality Over Quantity

In a world where social media thrives on numbers and popularity, the value of quality over quantity often gets lost in the pursuit of accumulating more connections. But amidst this digital cacophony, I found solace in embracing meaningful relationships over a vast social circle. This is a narrative of my journey, where I discovered the profound joy and fulfillment that comes from nurturing deep connections with a select few, rather than spreading myself thin in the quest for superficial popularity.

My Memoir###
It was during my college years that I first encountered the allure of quantity in social interactions. Surrounded by a myriad of faces, I initially believed that the more friends I had, the richer my social life would be. I busied myself with fleeting conversations, superficial gatherings, and the relentless pursuit of being known by as many people as possible. Yet, amidst the noise, I felt an inexplicable emptiness lingering within me.

It wasn't until a chance encounter with a group of individuals who valued depth over breadth that I began to reconsider my approach. They weren't concerned with the number of friends they had on social media or the size of their social gatherings. Instead, they prioritized meaningful connections, investing time and effort into nurturing relationships that enriched their lives.

Inspired by their philosophy, I made a conscious decision to shift my focus from quantity to quality. I began to invest more time in cultivating deep connections with a select few individuals who resonated with my values and aspirations. Through heartfelt conversations, shared experiences, and unwavering support, these relationships blossomed into something truly remarkable.

With each passing day, I discovered the beauty of vulnerability and authenticity in my interactions. No longer did I feel the pressure to maintain a facade or please everyone around me. Instead, I reveled in the comfort of being my true self, knowing that I was accepted and cherished for who I was.

Conclusion
In embracing quality over quantity, I found a profound sense of fulfillment and contentment that had eluded me for so long. Through the genuine connections I forged, I experienced moments of joy, laughter, and companionship that enriched my life in ways I could have never imagined.

While the allure of quantity may still linger in the periphery, I am steadfast in my commitment to cherishing meaningful relationships over a large social circle. For in the depth of these connections lies the true essence of human connection and the boundless beauty of the human experience.

Embrace Change: Adaptability is Key

Change – it's the one constant in life, isn't it? Sometimes it feels like life is a series of unpredictable twists and turns, throwing us off balance when we least expect it. But what if I told you that embracing change could be the key to unlocking your personal growth? It's all about adaptability – the ability to adjust and thrive in the face of uncertainty. Let me share with you a friend's personal story that illustrates just how powerful embracing change can be.

Friend's Tale

During the COVID-19 pandemic, many industries experienced economic downturns, leading to widespread layoffs. On a crisp autumn morning in 2020, Maya's life took an unexpected turn, forever altering its course. Having enjoyed years of stability in her career, she was suddenly confronted with the daunting reality of a layoff. Shock and uncertainty surged through her like an unrelenting tide, threatening to engulf her in a sea of fear and despair.

At first, Maya clung to the familiar like a shipwreck survivor clinging to driftwood, desperately yearning for a return to normalcy. But as days turned into weeks and the harsh truth of her situation settled in, she came to understand that resisting change was futile. If she was to navigate this storm, she knew she had to embrace adaptability.

With newfound determination, Maya embarked on a journey to welcome change rather than fight against it. She sought out opportunities to enhance her skills, networked with professionals across different industries, and explored paths she had never before considered. It was far from smooth sailing – moments of doubt and frustration punctuated her progress – yet with each step forward, Maya felt herself becoming stronger and more adaptable.

As the months passed, Maya began to reap the rewards of her perseverance. She secured a new job that not only challenged her but also allowed her to thrive in ways she had never imagined. Through this experience, Maya gleaned invaluable insights into the importance of adaptability and resilience in navigating life's twists and turns. Change ceased to be a dreaded adversary; instead, it became a catalyst for her personal growth and self-discovery.

Conclusion
So, to anyone facing uncertainty or undergoing a period of change, I urge you to embrace it with open arms. Remember that adaptability is not just a skill – it's a mindset. Instead of viewing change as a threat, see it as a chance to evolve and become the best version of yourself. It won't always be easy, but the rewards of embracing change far outweigh the comfort of staying stagnant. Trust in your ability to adapt, and you'll find that life's challenges become stepping stones to a brighter future.

Gratitude: Count the Blessings in Your Life

Amidst the flurry of our daily lives, it's all too easy to become entangled in the whirlwind of responsibilities, deadlines, and challenges. Amidst this chaos, however, lies a powerful antidote to stress and dissatisfaction: gratitude. Gratitude is the practice of acknowledging and appreciating the blessings, big and small, that enrich our lives every day. Allow me to share the Mahabharata story passed down by my grandfather, a tale often recounted during our summer vacations together.

Thatha's Kathai
From the ancient Indian epic, the Mahabharata. Draupadi, the wife of the Pandava princes, faced unimaginable trials and tribulations throughout her life. Yet, amidst the chaos of war and personal tragedy, she found solace in gratitude.

When asked by the sage Durvasa how she managed to stay resilient in the face of adversity, Draupadi replied, "I have learned to find beauty in even the darkest of moments, for they remind me of the light that shines within me and around me."

In today's fast-paced world, cultivating gratitude can seem like a daunting task. However, it need not be complicated. One simple yet powerful way to embrace gratitude is by keeping a gratitude journal.

Each day, take a few moments to reflect on the blessings that you've encountered, whether it's a kind gesture from a stranger or a moment of serenity in nature. Write down these moments of gratitude, allowing yourself to bask in their warmth and significance.

As you embark on this journey of gratitude, you may find that your perspective begins to shift. The challenges that once seemed insurmountable may appear more manageable, and moments of joy may become more abundant. Gratitude acts as a beacon of light, illuminating the path toward a more fulfilling and meaningful life.

Conclusion
Just as Draupadi found strength and resilience amidst adversity, so too can we find solace and joy in the blessings that surround us. Through the simple act of acknowledging and appreciating the abundance in our lives, we cultivate a spirit of gratitude that transforms not only ourselves but also the world around us. So, let us pause, reflect, and give thanks for the countless blessings that enrich our lives each day.

Setting Boundaries: Power of Saying No

In the fast-paced whirlwind of modern life, the art of setting boundaries has become indispensable for maintaining one's well-being. Whether it's in our personal or professional spheres, knowing when to gracefully decline and say "no" is crucial for safeguarding our mental and physical health. This essay delves into the significance of setting boundaries, drawing from personal anecdotes and insights.

A Personal Anecdote

Imagine a scenario where your workload is already towering, deadlines looming like dark clouds, and your inbox resembles a bottomless pit of unanswered emails. It was in such a moment that I found myself struggling to keep up with the incessant demands of work. The pressure was suffocating, and my sanity teetered on the edge of collapse.

In the midst of this chaos, a colleague approached me with an additional project, promising great rewards but demanding a significant investment of time and effort. My initial instinct was to accept, fearing the consequences of refusal—disappointment, judgment, or missed opportunities. However, in a rare moment of clarity, I realized the importance of setting boundaries.

Reflecting on past experiences, I recalled a time when I had overextended myself, sacrificing sleep, leisure, and even personal relationships in pursuit of professional success. The result? Burnout, anxiety, and a profound sense of emptiness.

It was a wake-up call—a reminder that my well-being should never be compromised for the sake of fleeting accolades or momentary gains. Armed with this realization, I politely declined the additional workload, explaining my current commitments and the need to prioritize tasks effectively.

To my surprise, my colleague understood and respected my decision, offering support rather than criticism. It was a pivotal moment—an affirmation that setting boundaries not only preserves one's well-being but also fosters mutual respect and understanding in relationships.

Conclusion
In a world where busyness is glorified and productivity is paramount, the ability to set boundaries is a radical act of self-care. It's about honoring your limitations, valuing your time, and nurturing a healthy balance between work and life.

As I navigate the labyrinth of existence, I remind myself of the power of "no"—a small word with immense potential to safeguard my well-being and preserve my sanity.

Remember, saying "no" doesn't make you selfish or incompetent; it makes you human. So, the next time you feel overwhelmed, don't hesitate to set boundaries, for it is in protecting yourself that you truly thrive.

Financial Planning: Securing Future

In the vast ocean of life, navigating towards a secure financial future requires a sturdy vessel: a well-thought-out financial plan. Just like a sailor prepares meticulously before embarking on a journey, so too must we prepare for the voyage of life. Let me take you on a journey through the importance of financial planning, drawing from personal experiences and insights.

Setting Sail: A Lesson from My Father

During my childhood, I vividly recall my father's meticulous approach to saving money. Despite our modest means, he made it a priority to set aside a portion of his earnings each month. Sitting at the kitchen table with bills spread out before him and a calculator in hand, he charted our family's financial path with unwavering dedication. His commitment wasn't merely about accumulating wealth; it was about paving a secure road for his children to navigate life's challenges with ease.

As we embarked on our professional journeys, the temptation to indulge in lavish spending often overshadowed the importance of saving. Dining out at fancy restaurants, splurging on gadgets, and spontaneous trips became the norm. However, amidst the allure of instant gratification, the essence of financial planning eluded us.

Investing in Retirement Funds: By allocating a portion of our income towards retirement funds, we not only harness the power of compounding but also mitigate the risk of outliving our savings. Whether through employer-sponsored Provident Fund (PF) schemes or individual retirement accounts (IRAs), starting to invest early and maintaining consistent contributions sets the stage for a comfortable retirement.

Building Savings Accounts: In tandem with retirement funds, cultivating savings accounts serves as a safety net for unforeseen expenses and long-term goals. Setting achievable targets and automating savings contributions streamlines the process, ensuring that we prioritize financial security amidst life's uncertainties.

From emergency funds to down payments for homes, savings accounts offer liquidity and flexibility, empowering us to navigate life's milestones with confidence. By adhering to a budget and distinguishing between needs and wants, we lay the foundation for a resilient financial future.

Marriage and Beyond The journey of financial planning extends beyond individual aspirations, encompassing shared goals and responsibilities in marriage.

Open communication, mutual respect, and collaborative decision-making form the bedrock of financial harmony. Through joint budgeting, setting common financial objectives, and aligning spending habits, couples can navigate the complexities of merging finances with ease.

Moreover, investing in insurance policies and estate planning safeguards against unforeseen adversities, ensuring continuity and security for loved ones.

Conclusion
In essence, financial planning transcends mere budgeting; it embodies a mindset of foresight, discipline, and empowerment. By embracing the principles of investing in retirement funds, cultivating savings accounts, and navigating life's transitions with prudence, we chart a course toward a prosperous tomorrow.

Remember, the journey of financial planning begins with a single step – a commitment to securing your tomorrow today. So, let us embark on this transformative journey together, empowered by knowledge, guided by wisdom, and enriched by the promise of a brighter future.

In the bustling streets of Hyderabad, amidst the clamor of honking horns and vibrant marketplaces, lies a truth that transcends time and age - the pursuit of knowledge knows no boundaries. It's a lesson I learned first hand, watching my grandmother navigate the intricacies of a smartphone with the curiosity of a child. In a world where technology evolves faster than the blink of an eye, the mantra of lifelong learning becomes not just a suggestion but a necessity for survival.

My Narrative###
I remember the day my grandmother, in her late seventies, gingerly picked up her first smartphone. She had spent most of her life without ever encountering such a device.

Yet, there she was, determined to unravel its mysteries. With patience as her guide, she embarked on a journey of discovery, tapping away at the screen with the tenacity of a seasoned explorer. In a matter of weeks, she transformed from a novice to a proficient user, effortlessly navigating apps and sending messages with the finesse of a digital native.

Her journey taught me a valuable lesson - age is merely a number when it comes to learning. Just as she embraced the challenge of mastering new technology, so too can we all embark on the path of continuous learning, no matter our age or background.

Learning Never Stops: In a country as diverse as India, where tradition meets modernity at every corner, the spirit of learning permeates through generations.

From mastering the art of traditional Indian cooking to delving into the intricacies of artificial intelligence, the thirst for knowledge knows no bounds.

Think back to a time when the internet was still in its infancy. We embarked on a journey of exploration, venturing into the digital realm with wide-eyed wonder. With each click of the mouse, we unlocked a world of possibilities, connecting with people and ideas from every corner of the globe.

And just when we thought we had it all figured out, smartphones emerged, ushering in a new era of connectivity and convenience. Once again, we adapted, embracing change with open arms and curious minds.

Conclusion
As I reflect on the lessons learned from my grandmother's journey and our collective experience with technology, one truth becomes abundantly clear - learning is not a destination but a lifelong journey. Whether we're mastering new technologies, exploring creative pursuits, or honing professional skills, the key to personal growth and success lies in our ability to embrace change and keep expanding our knowledge horizons.

So, let us pledge to be perpetual students of life, seizing every opportunity to learn and grow, for in the pursuit of knowledge, we discover the true essence of what it means to be human.

Release and Renew: Self-Forgiveness

In the quiet moments of introspection, when the weight of our mistakes threatens to suffocate us, there lies a beacon of hope - the power of self-forgiveness. It's a lesson I learned through the trials and tribulations of life, realizing that harboring guilt and blame only serves to imprison the soul. As we journey through the tapestry of existence, it becomes imperative to embrace our imperfections, for it is in forgiveness that true liberation resides.

My Memoir

There was a time in my life when I found myself consumed by remorse, haunted by the ghosts of my past actions. Every misstep, every wrong turn, seemed to echo in the corridors of my mind, a constant reminder of my fallibility. I carried the burden of my mistakes like a heavy cloak, allowing shame to dictate my self-worth.

It wasn't until I reached a breaking point, teetering on the edge of despair, that I realized the futility of my self-imposed punishment. In a moment of clarity, I made a conscious decision to release myself from the chains of guilt and embrace the possibility of redemption.

Learn to Forgive Yourself: In a world that often demands perfection, we find ourselves ensnared in a web of unrealistic expectations and unattainable standards. Yet, amidst the chaos and clamor, there exists a sanctuary of self-compassion, where forgiveness serves as the cornerstone of personal growth and healing.

How many times have we berated ourselves for past failures, replaying the same mistakes like a broken record? How many opportunities for growth and transformation have we squandered in the pursuit of self-flagellation? It is time to break free from the chains of self-doubt and embrace the transformative power of forgiveness.

Conclusion

As I stand on the precipice of self-discovery, I am reminded of the words of the great poet Rumi, who once said, "The wound is the place where the Light enters you." In our moments of deepest despair, it is often our wounds that lead us toward healing and wholeness. So let us cast aside the burden of guilt and shame, embracing our flaws and failures as catalysts for growth.

For in the act of forgiving ourselves, we pave the way for a brighter, more compassionate future, where grace and acceptance reign supreme. So, my dear friends, let us embark on this journey of self-forgiveness together, for in the acceptance of our imperfections, we discover the true essence of our humanity.

In the hustle and bustle of modern life, where time seems to slip through our fingers like grains of sand, there exists a profound truth - the power of the present moment. It's a lesson I learned through the crucible of adversity, realizing that life's most precious moments often unfold in the here and now.

As we navigate the maze of existence, it becomes increasingly important to cultivate a sense of mindfulness, anchoring ourselves in the present rather than dwelling on the past or fretting about the future.

My Chronicle
For the longest time, I found myself caught in the relentless pursuit of tomorrow, forever chasing the elusive promise of a brighter future. From meticulously crafted five-year plans to grandiose dreams of success and achievement, I was consumed by a singular obsession with what lay ahead. Little did I realize that in my relentless quest for tomorrow, I was missing out on the beauty and richness of today.

It wasn't until life threw me a curveball in the form of a cancer diagnosis and a series of near-death experiences that I was jolted out of my reverie. Suddenly, the future I had meticulously mapped out seemed like a distant mirage, and all that mattered was the preciousness of the present moment. In the quiet stillness of hospital rooms and the gentle caress of sunlight streaming through the window, I discovered a profound sense of gratitude for the gift of life itself.

Living in the Present: In a world that glorifies productivity and achievement, it's all too easy to lose sight of the simple joys that surround us each day. Yet, amidst the chaos and clamor of modernity, there exists a sanctuary of stillness and presence, where time slows down and the beauty of existence reveals itself in all its splendor.

Practicing mindfulness is not merely a fleeting trend but a timeless practice that has the power to transform our relationship with reality itself. Whether it's through the gentle rhythm of our breath or the soft caress of a gentle breeze, mindfulness invites us to anchor ourselves in the present moment, letting go of regrets from the past and anxieties about the future.

Conclusion

As I reflect on the lessons learned from my journey of self-discovery, one truth becomes abundantly clear - life is not a destination but a journey, and the only moment we truly have is the present. So let us embrace the now with open arms, savoring each moment as if it were our last, for in the richness of the present moment, we discover the true essence of what it means to be alive.

In the immortal words of the song from the Bollywood movie Kal Ho Naa Ho, "Har pal yahan jee bhar jiyo, jo hai samaa, kal ho na ho," which translates to "Live every moment to the fullest, for who knows if there will be a tomorrow."

Kindness: Power of Small Gestures

In the rich tapestry of human existence, woven with threads of joy and sorrow, there exists a universal language that transcends barriers of culture and creed - the language of kindness. It's a lesson ingrained in the very fabric of our being, echoed through the ages in tales of compassion and empathy.

As we navigate the complexities of modern life, it becomes increasingly clear that in a world often marred by strife and division, the simple act of kindness has the power to illuminate even the darkest of days.

An anecdote from Panchatantra
Centuries ago, in the ancient land of India, there lived a wise sage named Vishnu Sharma. Faced with the daunting task of imparting moral lessons to the young princes of a kingdom, he turned to the timeless wisdom of storytelling found in the Panchatantra.

Among the myriad tales that populate the pages of the Panchatantra, one stands out as a shining example of the transformative power of kindness. It is the story of a lion who, out of kindness, spares the life of a mouse who inadvertently disturbed his sleep.

Later, when the lion is ensnared in a hunter's net, the mouse returns the favor by gnawing through the ropes, setting the lion free. In that simple act of kindness, the lion and the mouse forge an unbreakable bond, proving that even the smallest creatures can make a big difference through their compassion.

Be Kind: In a world where the tumult of daily life often drowns out the gentle whispers of the heart, it's easy to lose sight of the profound impact that kindness can have on both the giver and the receiver. Yet, amidst the chaos and clamor, there exists a sanctuary of compassion and empathy, where even the simplest acts of kindness can blossom into profound moments of connection and understanding.

Whether it's offering a warm smile to a stranger, lending a helping hand to someone in need, or simply taking the time to listen with an open heart, kindness knows no bounds. It is a universal currency that transcends barriers of language and culture, weaving a tapestry of love and understanding that binds us all together as one human family.

Conclusion

As I reflect on the timeless wisdom of the Panchatantra and the myriad lessons it holds, one truth becomes abundantly clear - kindness is not merely a virtue but a way of life. It is a guiding light that illuminates our path, leading us toward a brighter, more compassionate future.

So let us pledge to be beacons of kindness in a world often shrouded in darkness, spreading love and light wherever we go. In the end, it is not the grand gestures or lofty ambitions that define us, but the simple acts of kindness that touch the hearts and souls of those around us.

Failing Forward: Success Stories

In the grand symphony of life, where the melody of success is often accompanied by the discordant notes of failure, there exists a profound truth - failure is not the end but merely a stepping stone on the path to greatness. It's a lesson exemplified by countless individuals throughout history, from humble beginnings to towering achievements. As we navigate the ebbs and flows of our own journeys, it becomes increasingly clear that the road to success is paved with setbacks and challenges, each failure serving as a valuable lesson in resilience and perseverance.

Real-Time Example: Sudha Murthy
In the bustling streets of India, amidst the cacophony of everyday life, there exists a beacon of hope and inspiration - Sudha Murthy, a renowned philanthropist and author known for her unwavering commitment to social causes. Born into a middle-class family in Karnataka, Sudha faced her fair share of challenges growing up. However, it was her resilience in the face of adversity that set her apart.

After completing her education, Sudha embarked on a journey to make a difference in the world. Inspired by her experiences and driven by a desire to create positive change, she co-founded Infosys Foundation, the philanthropic arm of Infosys, with her husband Narayana Murthy. The very same Infosys that once marked the beginning of my IT journey.

Despite facing numerous obstacles along the way, including skepticism from those who doubted her ability to succeed in a male-dominated industry, Sudha remained steadfast in her pursuit of creating positive change.

Throughout her career, Sudha encountered her fair share of failures and setbacks. Yet, rather than allowing them to deter her, she embraced each challenge as an opportunity for growth and learning. From failed initiatives to personal setbacks, Sudha approached each setback with humility and grace, using it as fuel to propel herself forward toward her goals.

Be it providing education to underprivileged children, empowering rural communities, or championing the cause of gender equality, Sudha Murthy's legacy serves as a testament to the transformative power of embracing failure. Her resilience, determination, and unwavering commitment to her principles have inspired countless individuals to persevere in the face of adversity and continue striving for a better tomorrow.

Embrace Failure: In a world that often glorifies success and achievement, it's easy to view failure as a mark of shame or inadequacy. Yet, amidst the pressure to succeed, there exists a hidden truth - failure is not the opposite of success but rather a crucial component of it. It is through our failures that we gain invaluable insights, develop resilience, and ultimately, achieve true greatness.

Whether it's launching a new business venture, pursuing a passion project, or navigating the complexities of personal relationships, failure is an inevitable part of the human experience. Rather than allowing it to crush our spirits, we must learn to embrace failure as a teacher, guiding us towards greater heights of achievement and fulfillment.

Conclusion
As I reflect on the lessons learned from Sudha Murthy's journey and the countless others who have turned setbacks into success stories, one truth becomes abundantly clear - failure is not the end but merely a detour on the road to greatness. So let us embrace failure with open arms, recognizing it not as a sign of defeat but as a catalyst for growth and transformation.

For in the crucible of failure, we discover our true strength, resilience, and determination. And it is through our willingness to confront failure head-on, learn from our mistakes, and continue striving towards our goals, that we ultimately pave the way for success.

Dare to Grow: Risk-Taking Journey

In the vast expanse of life, where the familiar shores of comfort beckon with their reassuring embrace, there exists a call to adventure - the call to take risks. It's a call that echoes through the corridors of our minds, urging us to step beyond the boundaries of the known and embrace the vast unknown. As we stand at the crossroads of opportunity and uncertainty, it becomes increasingly clear that it is only by taking risks that we can truly unlock our full potential and experience the exhilarating journey of personal growth.

A Personal Anecdote
My in-laws always dreamed of having both their sons reside in the same city due to age and travel constraints. My husband, being the younger one, settled in Mumbai, while his elder brother established himself in Bangalore. My husband and I attempted several times to secure jobs in Bangalore to fulfill this familial wish. While it was easier for me, being in IT, it posed some challenges for my husband, who worked in logistics.

Towards the end of 2017, my brother-in-law embarked on a new venture by opening a vegetarian restaurant. The endeavor required additional support to expand and open branches. Driven by our desire to fulfill my in-laws' wish for familial togetherness, we made the bold decision to step out of our comfort zones and support my brother-in-law's passion.

Leaving behind my husband's secure job and the familiarity of Mumbai, we embarked on a journey into the unknown, venturing into the world of entrepreneurship. With the backing of our families and a shared vision for the future, we wholeheartedly committed ourselves to the endeavor. It was my brother-in-law's dream, and we were determined to do whatever it took to help him realize it.

The journey was fraught with challenges. Navigating the complexities of the culinary world and managing the demands of running a business tested our resilience at every turn. Initially, we started as a hotel specializing in South Indian dishes, which quickly gained popularity. As we aimed to diversify and grow, we went ahead and partnered with Adyar Grand Sweets for franchising, Krishna Enterprises for packaged water and drinks, and Balaji Bakers for all baking products such as pizzas, samosas, veg puffs, cakes, and other varieties.

However, just as our restaurant began to gain momentum and carve out its place in the culinary scene, the COVID-19 pandemic struck. Overnight, our bustling eatery transformed into a shadow of its former self as lockdowns were enforced, and customers dwindled.

Faced with the harsh realities of an uncertain future, we made the difficult decision to pivot our business model. Collaborating with a partner, we transformed the restaurant into a cloud kitchen and returned to Mumbai. Though it was a setback, it did not diminish our resolve.

Drawing upon the lessons learned and the strength gained from our experiences, we embraced a new chapter in our lives with renewed determination. Returning to the familiarity of corporate life, we found ourselves inspired by the resilience of the human spirit and the transformative power of taking risks.

Conclusion
As I reflect on the tumultuous journey that led me from the heights of entrepreneurial ambition to the depths of uncertainty and back again, one truth becomes abundantly clear - taking risks is not merely about achieving success but about embracing the full spectrum of human experience.

Whether it's the thrill of pursuing a passion project or the resilience to bounce back from failure, taking risks is an essential catalyst for personal growth and self-discovery. And though our restaurant may have closed its doors, the lessons learned and the memories forged will forever remain etched in my heart as a testament to the transformative power of embracing the unknown.

In the bustling chaos of modern life, where we are constantly bombarded with information and distractions, the quest for peace of mind often seems elusive. However, the ancient wisdom of simplifying our lives can provide a profound sense of tranquility and clarity. The Panchatantra, a collection of ancient Indian fables, offers timeless lessons that emphasize the importance of simplicity and focus. One such story is that of "The Hermit and the Mouse," which illustrates how decluttering one's life can lead to greater peace and effectiveness.

The Hermit and the Mouse: A Panchatantra Tale
In a dense forest, there lived a hermit who had renounced worldly possessions to lead a life of meditation and simplicity. His only companion was a mouse that frequently gnawed at his few belongings. Frustrated, the hermit decided to use his powers to transform the mouse into a cat, thinking it would solve his problem. However, the cat was soon troubled by dogs. The hermit then transformed the cat into a dog, and later, the dog into a lion to protect it from further threats.

Ironically, the lion became a source of fear for the hermit himself, as it started to growl menacingly at him. Realizing that the transformations only added complexity and new problems, the hermit turned the lion back into a mouse. He understood that simplicity was the key to peace, and adding layers of complexity only distracted him from his spiritual path.

The Modern Pursuit of Simplicity: The story of the hermit and the mouse mirrors our own struggles with the clutter in our lives. Whether it is physical possessions, digital distractions, or emotional baggage, the accumulation of unnecessary items and commitments can overwhelm us. Simplifying our lives can lead to greater peace of mind and a more focused, fulfilling existence.

Decluttering for Peace of Mind: One effective way to simplify life is by decluttering our physical spaces. Adopting a minimalist lifestyle by donating unnecessary belongings can transform our living environments from chaotic to serene. This not only creates a more orderly space but also reduces the mental burden of keeping track of so many items.

For example, when I decided to declutter my home, I started with my wardrobe. I donated clothes that I hadn't worn in over years and kept only those that I truly needed and loved.

The process was liberating; it felt as though I was shedding unnecessary layers and making room for more meaningful experiences. This initial step inspired me to simplify other areas of my life, from my digital space—by deleting old files and unsubscribing from unwanted emails—to my daily schedule, by prioritizing tasks and eliminating non-essential activities.

Emotional and Mental Decluttering: Simplification is not limited to the physical realm. Decluttering our minds by practicing mindfulness and meditation can help clear mental fog and improve focus.
Letting go of grudges and past regrets is another powerful way to achieve emotional clarity. By focusing on the present moment and releasing negative emotions, we can cultivate a sense of inner peace.

Benefits of a Simplified Life: The benefits of simplifying are manifold. With fewer possessions to manage, we save time and reduce stress. A clean, organized space fosters a calm and creative mind. Emotionally, letting go of past burdens allows us to experience greater joy and contentment. Simplifying our lives can also lead to better relationships, as we become more present and attentive to those around us.

Conclusion
The timeless wisdom of the Panchatantra reminds us that simplicity is the key to a peaceful and fulfilling life.

By decluttering our physical spaces, minds, and emotions, we can reduce stress and increase our overall well-being. Just as the hermit in the story found peace by returning to simplicity, we too can find greater clarity and joy by embracing a minimalist approach to life. Simplify, and discover the profound tranquility that comes with living a life free from unnecessary burdens.

Embrace Growth Through Feedback

In the journey of personal and professional growth, feedback is a crucial yet often overlooked tool. As we age and accumulate experience, there is a tendency to believe we have all the answers. However, this mindset can create blind spots and limit our potential for improvement. Embracing feedback, especially constructive criticism, can help us refine our skills, enhance our relationships, and foster continuous growth.

My Experience with Feedback
I recall a time in my career when I believed I had reached a level of proficiency that made feedback unnecessary. Having worked in my field for several years, I felt confident in my methods and decisions. '

However, this confidence gradually turned into complacency. My performance plateaued, and I began noticing subtle changes in my workplace dynamics. My colleagues were less forthcoming with their thoughts, and team projects didn't flow as smoothly as before.

One day, during a team meeting, a junior colleague hesitantly suggested a different approach to a project I was leading. Initially, I felt defensive, thinking, "What could they possibly know that I don't?" But something in their tone made me pause.

I realized my reaction was not only dismissive but also counterproductive. It was then that I decided to actively seek feedback, regardless of the source. I approached my colleagues and asked for their honest opinions on my working style and areas where I could improve. The responses were eye-opening.

They highlighted that while my technical skills were strong, my communication style often came off as unapproachable and my decision-making process excluded valuable team input. This feedback was hard to hear, but it was also the catalyst I needed for change.

The Power of Feedback: Seeking feedback is not just about identifying weaknesses; it's about understanding how others perceive us and finding ways to bridge gaps in our knowledge and behavior. Feedback can reveal insights we might be blind to and provide a roadmap for personal and professional development.

In the workplace, feedback can enhance performance by highlighting areas for improvement and confirming what we do well. For instance, after receiving feedback from my colleagues, I made a conscious effort to improve my communication and include more team input in the decision-making process. The change was noticeable. Team morale improved, and our projects were more collaborative and successful.

In personal relationships, feedback helps us understand how our actions affect others. By seeking feedback from family and friends, we can learn to be more empathetic and responsive to their needs, thus strengthening our relationships.

How to Seek and Handle Feedback:
1. Be Open and Receptive: Listen with an open mind, focusing on growth rather than defending yourself.
2. Ask Specific Questions: Request feedback on particular aspects of your performance or behavior for more actionable insights.
3. Choose the Right Time and Place: Select a conducive environment for honest feedback, avoiding stressful or high-pressure situations.
4. Reflect and Act: Reflect on the feedback, identify improvement areas, and create an action plan.
5. Follow Up: Regularly check in with those who provided feedback to track your progress and show your commitment to growth

Conclusion
As we age and grow in our careers and personal lives, the value of feedback cannot be overstated. It helps us maintain a growth mindset, improve our performance, and build stronger relationships. My own experience taught me that seeking feedback, even when it's uncomfortable, is essential for continuous improvement.

By embracing constructive criticism, we can overcome our blind spots and unlock our full potential. So, be open, ask for feedback, and let it guide you toward a path of ongoing growth and success.

In life, amidst the rush and commotion, finding our true purpose can often feel like searching for a needle in a haystack. We follow routines and meet expectations, yet often overlook the essential question: What truly fulfills us? This journey of self-discovery often comes through profound experiences. I invite you to embark on a voyage through my story, intertwined with the pursuit of purpose and the joy of giving back.

A Turning Point

Like many others, I was on a conventional path. I followed the expected trajectory: school, career, and the quest for success. My life was a series of checkboxes, and I believed that ticking them off would lead to happiness. I worked hard, climbed the corporate ladder, and amassed accolades, yet something was always missing. I ignored the subtle signs of dissatisfaction, pushing them aside with the hope that the next achievement would bring the fulfillment I sought.

Then, my world came to a screeching halt. I was diagnosed with cancer. The news hit me like a freight train, shaking the very foundations of my existence. Suddenly, the career I had worked so hard to build seemed insignificant in the face of my mortality.

As I navigated through treatments, doctor visits, and endless waiting rooms, I had ample time to reflect on my life. I realized that I had been living on autopilot, prioritizing societal expectations over my own happiness.

Discovering Purpose: Amidst the turmoil of treatments and uncertainty, I found solace in unexpected places. Volunteering for cancer support groups became my refuge, a sanctuary where I found connection and purpose. As I listened to the stories of fellow warriors and shared my own, a profound realization dawned: true fulfillment lies in giving back. It was this epiphany that led me to channel my efforts into supporting a cause greater than myself.

Silver Linings: Supporting a Noble Cause
In the midst of my journey, another chapter unfolded: the creation of "Silver Linings." This book, born from the depths of my experiences, serves as a beacon of hope for those navigating their own storms. But its significance extends beyond its pages. All proceeds from "Silver Linings" support an NGO dedicated to supporting children with cancer. Through the act of storytelling, we not only find healing but also contribute to a cause that touches countless lives.

Conclusion
Each individual's journey to discovering their purpose is singular and extraordinary.

It may unfold through challenges, as it did for me, or blossom from a deep-rooted passion or hobby. Whether by dedicating time to volunteering, expressing creativity, or engaging in philanthropy, we all possess the capacity to enact positive change. Let's respond to this inner call to action, attuned to the subtle stirrings within our hearts, and wholeheartedly embrace the voyage of self-discovery. Through this pursuit, we not only find personal fulfillment but also plant the seeds of optimism for a brighter future.

Embracing Meaningful Relationship Connections

In the whirl and rush of our daily lives, it's easy to overlook one of life's most precious treasures: relationships. Whether it's with our partners, parents, siblings, friends, or even our pets, the bonds we forge with others shape our experiences and enrich our lives in profound ways. Reflecting on my own journey, I've come to realize the immense value of investing time and energy into nurturing these connections. Allow me to share a small anecdote that underscores this importance.

My Recollection###
A couple of years back, in the midst of a busy workday, one of my colleagues received a devastating call informing him of his spouse's sudden passing in a tragic accident. Witnessing the profound impact it had on him, I couldn't help but reflect on my own relationship. Amidst the chaos of work deadlines and personal commitments, I realized I had been taking my partner for granted. Our once vibrant connection had dimmed under the weight of daily pressures.

Recognizing the growing distance between us, we made a conscious decision to prioritize our relationship by instituting a weekly date night—a dedicated time free from distractions and responsibilities.

Though carving out this time amidst our hectic schedules posed a challenge, we soon discovered its transformative power. Whether it was a quiet dinner at home or an adventurous outing, these regular date nights became the cornerstone of our relationship, reigniting the spark of companionship and strengthening our bond.

Investing Time and Energy in Relationships: This experience taught me a valuable lesson: relationships require intentional effort to thrive. Just as neglected plants wither without proper care, so too do our connections falter when neglected.

Whether it's scheduling regular phone calls with distant family members, planning weekend getaways with friends, or simply spending quality time with our pets, every investment in relationships pays dividends in the form of love, support, and companionship.

Consider the relationship with our parents, for instance. As we grow older and embark on our own paths, it's easy to take their presence for granted. Yet, taking the time to express gratitude, share meaningful conversations, or participate in shared activities can strengthen the bonds between generations and create lasting memories.

Similarly, nurturing relationships with siblings fosters a sense of camaraderie and solidarity that can weather life's storms. Whether through shared interests, inside jokes, or heartfelt conversations, the support of siblings enriches our lives in countless ways.

And let's not forget the importance of friendships—the family we choose for ourselves. By investing time and energy into these relationships, whether through regular meetups, spontaneous adventures, or simply lending a listening ear, we create a network of support that sustains us through life's ups and downs.

Conclusion
In a world that often prioritizes productivity and achievement, it's easy to overlook the simple yet profound joy of human connection. Yet, as my own experiences have taught me, nurturing relationships is essential for our emotional well-being and fulfillment.

Whether it's through regular date nights with our partners, heartfelt conversations with our parents, playful moments with siblings, or cherished memories with friends, investing time and energy into meaningful connections enriches our lives in ways that surpass material success. So let us not take these relationships for granted, but rather, cultivate them with care, knowing that in the tapestry of life, it is the bonds we forge with others that truly define our existence.

Recognizing and Celebrating Achievements

In our fast-paced world, it's easy to become ensnared in the whirlwind of daily activities, often overshadowing our accomplishments, whether significant or minor. However, taking the time to acknowledge and celebrate these moments is crucial for maintaining motivation, building self-esteem, and fostering a positive outlook. Whether it's treating yourself to a nice dinner after reaching a milestone or simply taking a moment to appreciate your progress, celebrating accomplishments is a practice that enriches our lives.

A Personal Journey of Celebrations

From a young age, I learned the importance of celebrating even the smallest of victories. I remember the thrill of winning my first table tennis match in school. It wasn't a major tournament, just an inter-school competition, but to me, it was monumental. My parents took me out for ice cream that evening, and that small gesture of celebration made me feel like a champion.

It taught me that acknowledging achievements, no matter how minor they may seem, can have a lasting impact on one's confidence and motivation.

School and College Victories During my college years, I continued to play table tennis, and the victories, though not always at national levels, were frequent enough to warrant celebration.

Each win, celebrated with friends or a quiet evening of reflection, reinforced my dedication and love for the sport. These moments were not just about the wins themselves, but about recognizing the hard work, perseverance, and growth that led to them.

Celebrating Academic and Professional Milestones
One of the most significant celebrations in my life was graduating with an Executive MBA. This milestone was a testament to years of hard work, sleepless nights, and relentless determination.

To celebrate, I treated myself to a wonderful dinner at my favorite restaurant. It was a moment of indulgence that felt richly deserved, a way to honor the effort and commitment that had brought me to that point.

First Abroad Trip and Dream Home Traveling abroad for the first time was another milestone that called for celebration. It was a dream come true, a testament to years of planning and saving. The sense of achievement was palpable as I stood in a foreign land, experiencing new cultures and sights.

Similarly, buying a house in Mumbai was a lifelong dream realized. The celebration for this was particularly sweet, as it represented years of hard work, dedication, and careful planning. It wasn't just a house; it was a symbol of perseverance and ambition.

Becoming an Author Another proud moment was when I published my first book in just five days, officially becoming an amateur author. The thrill of seeing my name on the cover and the positive feedback from readers was overwhelming.

To celebrate, I held a small gathering with close friends and family. Their support and encouragement made the achievement even more special.

Becoming a Fur Parent It brought immense joy and required its own form of celebration. Adopting a pet was a big decision, but the companionship and love that followed were unmatched. Celebrating this new addition to my life involved spending quality time with my new furry friend, and acknowledging the happiness and fulfillment they brought into my life.

Celebrating Family and Community Milestones
Celebrating 50 years of marriage for my in-laws was another profound moment. It was not just a celebration of their love and commitment, but also a reminder of the support and stability that family provides. The event was marked with a grand celebration, bringing together friends and family to honor their journey.

Additionally, my first donation of royalties from my book "Silver Linings" to an NGO was a moment of immense pride. Knowing that my work could contribute to a greater cause was incredibly fulfilling. This celebration was a quiet one, marked by a sense of contentment and purpose.

Conclusion
Celebrating accomplishments, whether they are personal milestones, professional achievements, or moments of giving back, enriches our lives and fuels our journey forward. It is through these celebrations that we acknowledge our efforts, cherish our progress, and inspire ourselves to aim higher.

Every victory, big or small, deserves to be recognized and celebrated, as these moments are the building blocks of a fulfilling and motivated life. So, take a moment to celebrate your accomplishments and cherish the journey they represent.

Passion Pursuits: Finding Fulfillment

In a world that often feels like a whirlwind of responsibilities and obligations, it's easy to let our passions fall by the wayside. However, carving out time for hobbies and interests that ignite our souls is essential for maintaining a sense of fulfillment and joy in life. Drawing inspiration from the pursuits of those around us, from family members to friends, we can embark on our own journey of pursuing passion projects. Let's explore how indulging in activities that align with our deepest interests can enrich our lives.

Small Tale
In my own familial circle, I've witnessed the transformative power of passion projects firsthand. After retiring, my mother decided to reignite her love for music by taking up music lessons. Despite years away from formal practice, her dedication and enthusiasm for learning filled our home with melodies once again.

Similarly, my sister, amidst the chaos of raising a family, always finds time to indulge in her passion for painting, whether it's through intricate pencil sketches or vibrant canvas creations. As for myself, I've discovered solace and connection through singing on a karaoke app and participating in musical meetups, where melodies intertwine to form a tapestry of shared experiences.

Furthermore, my father-in-law, following his voluntary retirement, delved into the intricate realms of Vedic studies and Sanskrit, finding profound fulfillment in unraveling the ancient wisdom encapsulated within these texts.

Even amidst his busy schedule, my husband makes it a priority to explore the world through local adventures and international travels, feeding his curiosity and thirst for new experiences. Meanwhile, my mother-in-law's passion for cooking has evolved into a culinary journey of experimentation and creativity, where every dish tells a story of love and tradition.

Conclusion
In essence, pursuing passion projects is not merely a luxury but a necessity for nurturing our souls and maintaining a balanced life. Whether it's through music, art, travel, or scholarly pursuits, these endeavors infuse our days with purpose and vitality.

By observing the passions of those around us and embracing our own unique interests, we open ourselves up to a world of endless possibilities and profound fulfillment. So, let's make a commitment to prioritize our passions, for in doing so, we cultivate a life that is rich in meaning and joy.

Life is an unpredictable journey filled with twists and turns, challenges, and unexpected opportunities. From navigating changes in financial status to relocating to different countries, each experience presents its own set of hurdles and triumphs.

Throughout my own life, I've encountered numerous trials. Yet, amidst these adversities, I've learned the invaluable lessons of staying positive and remaining flexible in the face of uncertainty. Let's explore how cultivating optimism and adaptability can empower us to thrive in any circumstance.

Personal Anecdote
My journey has been marked by moments of profound change and resilience. After experiencing significant financial losses, I found myself grappling with uncertainty and fear. However, instead of succumbing to despair, I chose to adopt a positive outlook, focusing on the lessons learned and the potential for growth. This shift in perspective not only helped me weather the storm but also paved the way for new opportunities to emerge.

Similarly, relocating to different countries brought its own set of challenges, including adapting to unfamiliar cultures and being away from loved ones. Despite the initial feelings of isolation and homesickness, I embraced the opportunity to explore new horizons and expand my worldview.

By staying flexible and open-minded, I discovered hidden treasures in every corner of the world, forging meaningful connections and enriching experiences along the way.

One of the most profound tests of positivity and flexibility came with the loss of my best friend to the same cancer that I had battled and survived. In the face of unimaginable grief, I chose to honor her memory by cherishing the precious moments we shared and finding solace in the belief that she lives on in spirit. Though the pain of her absence lingers, I draw strength from her enduring legacy and the love that continues to bind us together.

Conclusion
In life, we are bound to encounter obstacles and detours that challenge our resolve and test our resilience. Yet, it is during these moments of adversity that the power of positivity and flexibility shines brightest.

By cultivating optimism in every situation and embracing the unexpected with an open heart, we empower ourselves to navigate life's ups and downs with grace and courage. So, let us embrace the journey with unwavering hope and a willingness to adapt, knowing that even in the darkest of times, the light of possibility always shines through.

Age Gracefully: Beauty Within

As the years unfold, so too do the inevitable changes that accompany the journey of aging. From the emergence of gray hairs to the etching of wrinkles upon our skin, each transformation serves as a testament to the richness and depth of our life experiences. Yet, embracing aging goes beyond mere acceptance; it is an invitation to celebrate the wisdom and vitality that come with each passing year. Drawing inspiration from personal experiences and the wisdom of those who have walked the path before us, let us explore the beauty of embracing the inevitability of aging.

My Journey###
Approaching the milestone of 40, I found myself grappling with a mix of emotions, from nostalgia for the carefree days of youth to a sense of apprehension about the passage of time. Yet, as I reflect on the journey thus far, I am reminded that age is but a number, and true vitality springs from within. Instead of dreading the labels that come with aging, such as being called "Aunty" instead of "Akka,"

I choose to embrace the opportunity to redefine what it means to be 40. After all, as the saying goes, "40 is the new 20," a reminder that life is a continuous journey of growth and transformation.

In this journey of embracing aging, I find inspiration in the youthful spirit of my maternal uncle and aunt. Despite the passage of time and the onset of gray hairs and wrinkles, their zest for life remains undiminished.

Whether it's embarking on spontaneous adventures or simply sharing a hearty laugh over a cup of tea, they exemplify the beauty of staying young at heart. Their unwavering optimism and enthusiasm serve as a beacon of hope, reminding me that age is but a state of mind, and true beauty lies in embracing the full spectrum of life's experiences.

Conclusion
In a society that often idolizes youth and perpetuates unrealistic standards of beauty, embracing aging is an act of rebellion against the tyranny of ageism. It is a declaration that every laugh line and gray hair is a badge of honor, a testament to a life well-lived and lessons learned.

As we journey through the seasons of life, let us celebrate the inevitability of aging, knowing that true beauty radiates from within and that each passing year brings with it the gift of wisdom and grace. So, let us embrace the wrinkles and gray hairs with open arms, for they are symbols of a life lived fully and richly, and a reminder that the best is yet to come.

Recapitulation

1. Self-Acceptance: Embrace your uniqueness and imperfections.

2. Prioritize Health: Invest in both physical and mental well-being.

3. Quality Over Quantity: Foster meaningful relationships over a large social circle.

4. Embrace Change: Adaptability leads to personal growth and fulfillment.

5. Gratitude: Appreciate the blessings in your life daily.

6. Set Boundaries: Know when to say no for your own well-being.

7. Financial Planning: Start planning for your future financial security.

8. Continuous Learning: Expand your knowledge and skills throughout life.

9. Forgive Yourself: Learn from mistakes and move forward with grace.

10. Live in the Present: Stay mindful and grounded in the present moment.

11. Be Kind: Small acts of kindness can make a big difference.

12.   Embrace Failure: Failure is a stepping stone to
       success and growth.

13.   Take Risks: Step out of your comfort zone for
       personal growth.

14.   Simplify: Declutter your life for peace and clarity of
       mind.

15.   Seek Feedback: Be open to constructive criticism for
       personal improvement.

16.   Nurture Relationships: Invest time and effort into
       meaningful connections

17.   Find Purpose: Discover what truly fulfills and drives
       you.

18.   Celebrate Accomplishments: Acknowledge and
       celebrate your achievements.

19.   Pursue Passion Projects: Make time for hobbies and
       interests that bring you joy.

20.   Stay Positive and Flexible: Embrace life's
       uncertainties with optimism and adaptability.

21.   Embrace Aging: Accept and appreciate the natural
       process of aging as a part of life's journey.

Cause for a lifetime

For a Lifetime Cause: All proceeds from this book will be dedicated to the Rohit Memorial Trust indefinitely.

About the NGO

The Rohit Memorial Trust founded in 2008, has one of its major initiatives targeted towards serving children and youth, especially from the underprivileged sections of society, cancer-afflicted persons and their families, and terminally ill patients.

The Trust is registered for undertaking CSR activities vide Registration number CSR0004730 and is also registered to exempt donations by individuals under Section 80(G) of the Income Tax Act vide Registration No.54/2008-09.

Link: www.rohitmemorialtrust.org

Thank You Note

Dear All,

Thank you from the bottom of my heart for your invaluable help and support with my book. Your dedication and encouragement have meant the world to me. I am deeply grateful for your time, effort, and friendship. With your assistance, this book has truly blossomed, and this journey has been all the more special.

With heartfelt gratitude,
Aishwarya

~~~~~~

Dear Meenakshi & Team,

I wanted to express my heartfelt gratitude for allowing me the opportunity to collaborate with the Rohit Memorial Trust and donate the earnings from my book. Your support means a great deal to me, and I am honored to contribute to such a meaningful cause.

Thank you once again for your generosity and trust.

Warm regards,
Aishwarya
~~~~~~